Life-Size Baby Dinosaurs

by Kelly Milner Halls
illustrated by Adam Relf

RP | KIDS
PHILADELPHIA · LONDON

To my "babies," Kerry and Vanessa; so glad I got to care for you before you left the nest! To Lisa, Ronnie, and Jill; and to Charlie and Florence Magovern at the Stone Company (who shared their egg-cellent expertise).—K. M. H.

Text copyright © 2012 by Kelly Milner Halls
Illustrations copyright © 2012 by Adam Relf

Printed in China

Books published by Running Press are available at special discounts for bulk purchases in the United States by corporations, institutions, and other organizations. For more information, please contact the Special Markets Department at the Perseus Books Group, 2300 Chestnut Street, Suite 200, Philadelphia, PA 19103, or call (800) 810-4145, ext. 5000, or e-mail special.markets@perseusbooks.com.

ISBN 978-0-7624-4402-1
Library of Congress Control Number: 2011931419

E-book ISBN 978-0-7624-4512-7

9 8 7 6 5 4 3 2 1
Digit on the right indicates the number of this printing

Cover and interior design by Ryan Hayes
Edited by Lisa Cheng
Typography: Block and Billy

Published by Running Press Kids
An Imprint of Running Press Book Publishers
A Member of the Perseus Books Group
2300 Chestnut Street
Philadelphia, PA 19103-4371

Visit us on the web!
www.runningpress.com

Did you know prehistoric dinosaurs hatched from eggs? They started out small, even if they grew to be very large. How small? You're about to find out, so let's get cracking!

Psittacosaurus

(sih-TAK-oh-saw-rus) "parrot lizard"

Mother *Psittacosaurus* laid her eggs, each the size of a potato.

But baby *Psittacosaurus* was the size of an action figure.

When it was two years old, it weighed less than three pounds and might have had quills like a porcupine on its tail.

Oviraptor

(OH-vi-RAP-tore) "egg thief"

Mother *Oviraptor* laid her eggs, each the size of a hot dog bun.

But baby *Oviraptor* was the size of a brick.

Its mother may have fed it tiny bits of shellfish meat.

Saltasaurus

(sal-toe-SAW-rus) "lizard from Salta"

Mother *Saltasaurus* laid her eggs, each the size of a grapefruit.

But baby *Saltasaurus* was the size of a squirrel.

In time, it grew thick armored skin like a crocodile from tiny baby bumps.

Parasaurolophus

(pair-ah-sawr-oh-LAWF-us) "near crested lizard"

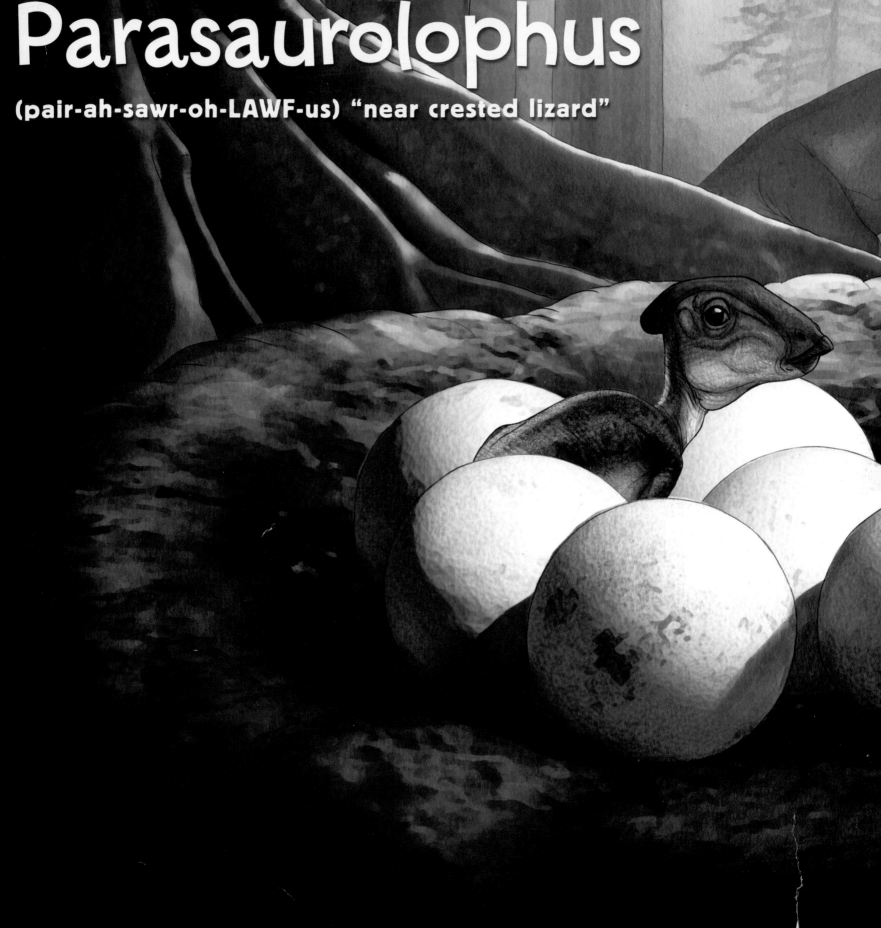

Mother *Parasaurolophus* may have laid her eggs, each the size of an orange.

But baby *Parasaurolophus* was probably the size of a pickle.

Its crest was small, but eventually grew long and useful.

Protoceratops

(pro-toe-SARE-ah-tops) "first horned face"

Mother *Protoceratops* laid her eggs, each the size of a water balloon.

But baby *Protoceratops* was the size of a candy bar.

It snuggled in its bowl-shaped nest with brothers and sisters, for a time.

Stegosaurus

(steg-o-SAWR-us) "roof lizard"

Mother *Stegosaurus* probably laid her eggs,
each the size of a softball.

But baby *Stegosaurus* was the size of kitten.

Weeks later, its feet were no bigger than a quarter.

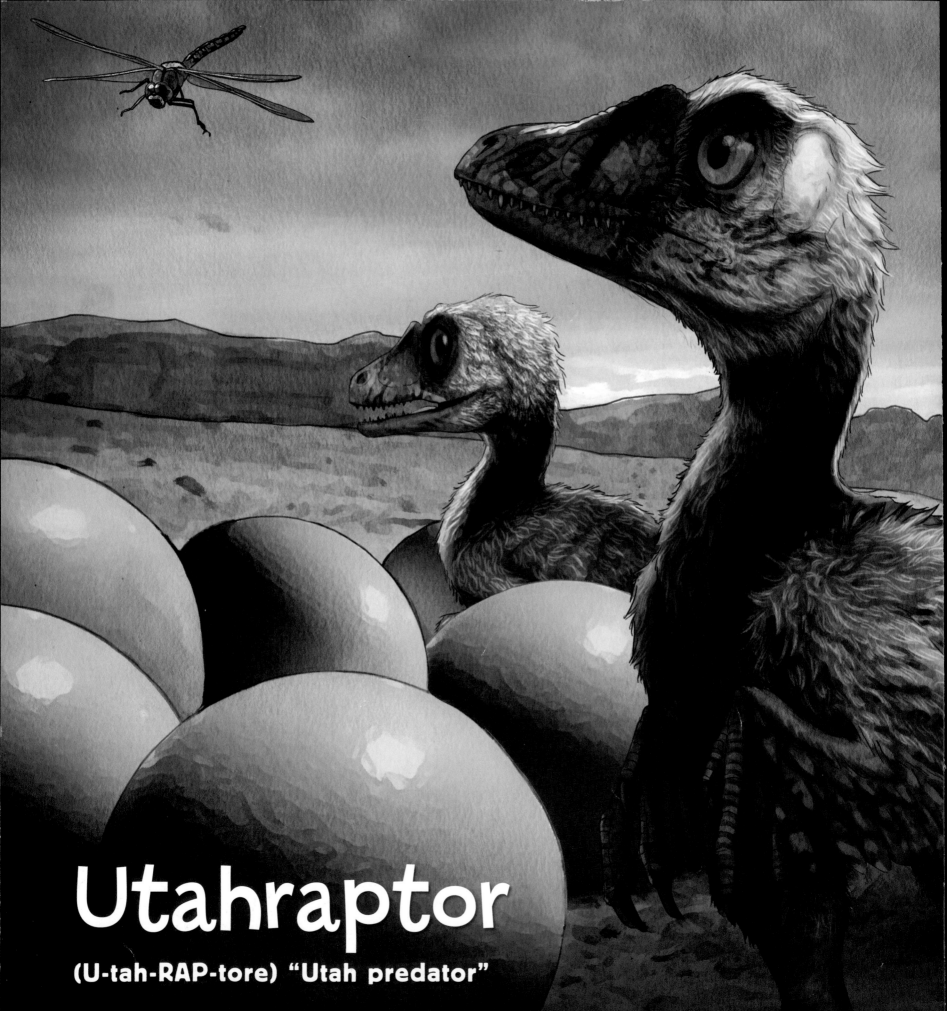

Utahraptor

(U-tah-RAP-tore) "Utah predator"

Mother *Utahraptor* may have laid her eggs, each the size of a small loaf of bread.

But baby *Utahraptor* was probably the size of a toy truck.

It ate insects before it learned to hunt.

Nodosaurus

(no-doe-SAWR-us) "Knob lizard"

Mother *Nodosaurus* may have laid her eggs, each the size of a balloon.

But baby *Nodosaurus* was the size of a baby doll.

These hatchlings stayed together until they doubled in size.

Maiasaura
(MY-ah-SAWR-ah) "good mother lizard"

Mother *Maiasaura* laid her eggs, each the size of an ostrich egg.

But baby *Maiasaura* was the size of a beach ball.

These tiny hatchlings couldn't walk at all, so mom and dad brought them food.

Tyrannosaur

(tie-ran-oh-SAWR) "tyrant lizard"

Mother *Tyrannosaur* laid her eggs, each the size of a football.

But baby *Tyrannosaur* was the size of an adult cat.

In just two years, it grew as big as a golden retriever.

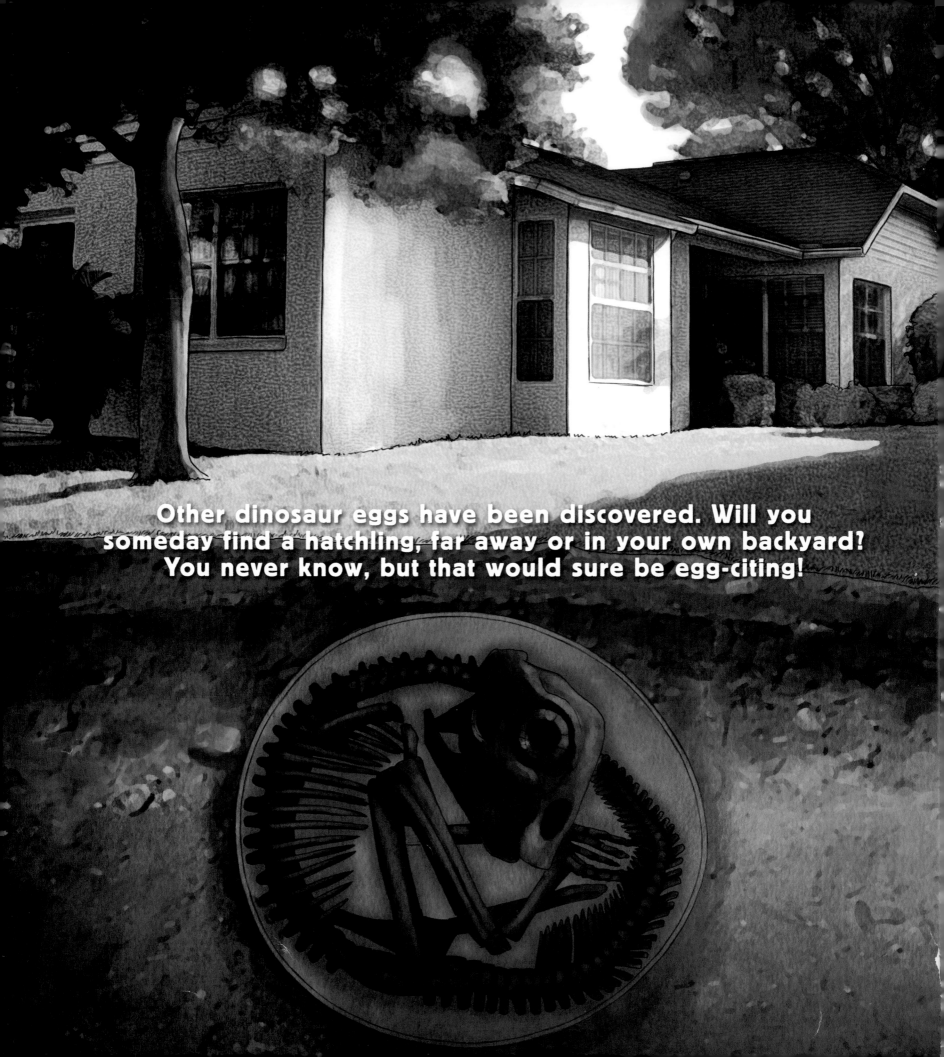

Other dinosaur eggs have been discovered. Will you someday find a hatchling, far away or in your own backyard? You never know, but that would sure be egg-citing!